The Bubble Machine

Text
Jean-Pierre Guillet

Illustrations
Gilles Tibo

Translated by Frances Morgan

CLEMENTINE'S KINGDOM

ECOLOGICAL TALES

QUINTIN
PUBLISHERS

Canadian Cataloguing in Publication Data

Guillet, Jean-Pierre

[Machine à bulles. English]

The bubble machine
(Ecological tales)

Translation of: La machine à bulles.
For children.

ISBN 2-89435-033-3 (bound) - ISBN 2-89435-034-1 (pbk.)

I. Tibo, Gilles, 1951- . II. Title. III. Title:
Machine à bulles. English. IV. Series.

PS8563.U546M3213 1994 jC843'.54 C94-940253-2
PS9563.U546M3213 1994
PZ27.B84Bu 1994

Design: Le groupe Flexidée

P.O. Box 340, Waterloo, Québec
Canada J0E 2N0
Tel.: (514) 539-3775

The publisher greatly appreciates the financial assistance received from the Canada Council and the Québec Ministry of Cultural Affairs for the production of this book.

Printed in Hong Kong

ISBN 2-89435-033-3 (Hardcover) 10 9 8 7 6 5 4 3 2 1
ISBN 2-89435-034-1 (Softcover) 10 9 8 7 6 5 4 3 2 1

To all children
on Earth

In a quiet country far, far from here, lives good King Pip and his daughter Clementine. One fine summer's day, Princess Clementine and her friends were blowing soap bubbles in the castle courtyard. The king was strolling nearby, admiring the flowers that lined the paths. Suddenly, a huge, rainbow-coloured bubble landed on his nose and burst. King Pip and his daughter laughed. "Sire Daddy," Clementine said, "show me how to catch bubbles and keep them from bursting."

"Impossible, my dear," replied the king. "There are a great many things of beauty that you can never hold in your hands."

Mook Chook, the magician-turned-gardener, had heard everything. How he would like to impress the king! He hurried to his workshop and shut himself up inside. Very soon, sounds could be heard behind the door. Ping! Bang! Whoosh! A strange smell filled the air and puffs of yellow smoke drifted out through the closed shutters.

"What is Mook Chook doing in there?" wondered the people in the castle. A very curious Clementine listened at the door. She wanted to discover his magic formula! "Abracada... pyja... choc...!" Rats! The magician's voice was too low. Clementine would never learn his secret.

Two days later, a triumphant Mook Chook finally emerged from his workshop. In front of a crowd of curious onlookers, he presented Clementine with a large round box, full of holes. "Now, turn the handle," he told her, smiling broadly.

Oh! The beautiful yellow bubbles! They flew to the right, they flew to the left, they floated higher and disappeared in the branches of the trees.

Enchanted, Clementine reached out and caught one, very carefully, as it drifted by. Her wish had come true! The little bubble didn't burst. It felt smooth and cool, as light as the wind.

In great excitement, Clementine turned the handle, again and again. A myriad of tiny suns twirled in the breeze and floated gently up into the air. What a beautiful sight! The princess gazed up at the sky. "It looks like a big, blue meadow," she thought to herself. "The clouds are little white sheep and I am feeding them golden popcorn."

All Clementine's friends crowded around for their chance to try the bubble machine. What a marvellous invention! "I want every home in the kingdom to have one," King Pip decreed.

"Quick!" he ordered Mook Chook. "Go back to work. My soldiers will help you. Every child must be able to make bubbles that will not burst."

The magician returned to his workshop. This time, he left the windows open, and everyone could watch the soldiers making the round boxes with holes. Mook Chook himself remained huddled in a corner, pouring chemicals from vials into huge copper cauldrons. The mixtures started to boil. Soon, steam rose from the pots and snatches of magic spells could be heard: “Abracada... pyja... nonono!
Abracada... choc... Eureka!”

Finally! The boxes were ready. Mook Chook filled them with a foaming yellow liquid for making bubbles. Soldiers travelled throughout the kingdom distributing boxes. Children and grown-ups blew bubbles to their hearts' content. From every yard, thousands of bubbles that would never burst drifted gently up into the sky.

Clementine and her father were admiring the sight from the castle ramparts. Suddenly, she asked, "But, Sire Daddy, what will happen to all these bubbles in the sky that will never burst ?"

"Hmmm... I do not know...," King Pip replied. "I suppose they will remain hanging in the air, that's all."

"Won't they block the sky ?"

"The sky is much too vast," the king laughed. "No one could ever make enough bubbles to fill it up."

However, little by little, the colour of the sky changed. Millions of tiny bubbles had formed a huge yellow dome over the kingdom.

"It's so hot!" Clementine complained one day.

"Nonsense! It's nothing," her father replied. "You know, I think I'll even go sun-bathing this morning." And down he went to the terrace to stretch out in his handsome bathing suit. A short time later, he was back in his chambers, as red as a lobster!

"Ouch! That hurts!" he groaned. "I've got a terrible sunburn. I should have put up the umbrella!"

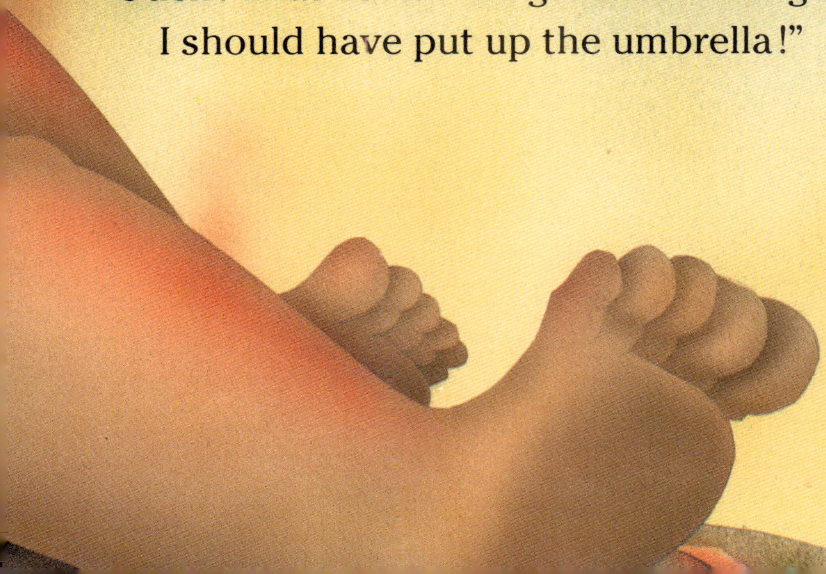

Then, bad news started pouring in from all over the kingdom. In the North, the ice was melting and causing floods. In the South, it was snowing. In the West, there was no rain and the crops were withering in the fields. In the East, there was acid rain. It was stinging people's skin and ruining their houses!

"So many disasters," the king lamented. "The climate has gone berserk. What will become of us ?"

"Sire Daddy, I'm sure it must be the bubbles !" Clementine exclaimed. "Let's go and ask Mook Chook."

In the magician's workshop, the princess noticed some bottles marked with a skull and crossbones. "Mook Chook," roared her father, "you have been sending poison up into the air ! You had better find a way to clean up the sky, and fast !"

"Yes, yes, forgive me, Sire, I did not do it on purpose," Mook Chook stammered.

For days, Mook Chook searched for a solution. He asked the king's archers to shoot arrows into the bubbles. Impossible, they had drifted too high. He sent up trained pigeons to prick them. But all the birds came back sick.

Finally, he invented bubble vacuum cleaners mounted on hot air balloons. "Sire," he said to King Pip, "now your soldiers can clean up the sky. With my invention, they will be able to reconvert the bubbles into liquid."

The soldiers went to work. Clementine and her father climbed to the top of the tallest tower in the castle to watch the operation. Hurray! It was working! Gradually, the sky became blue again!

After a great many trips back and forth in the hot air balloons, the soldiers brought Mook Chook huge bottles full of yellow poison. "Get rid of that filth once and for all!" ordered the king. The magician stroked his moustache. What could he do with all that awful liquid? He searched and searched.... Despite all his magic spells, none could provide him with a solution.

Meanwhile, King Pip ordered all his subjects to deposit their bubble machines at the side of the road. His soldiers would pick them up. And Mook Chook would just have to find another use for them! Poor Mook Chook! His troubles weren't over yet. How could he use all those discarded bubble machines?

One fine morning, he awoke with a cry of "Eureka!" and rushed to offer his sovereign one of the bubble machines. With a ceremonial flourish, he turned the handle. Beautiful music floated out.

"A music box! What a marvellous idea!" exclaimed the king. "That solves the problem of the boxes," the magician said to himself. "Now what am I going to do with all that poison?" Mook Chook is still looking for the answer!

Clementine, meanwhile, was happy to have her blue meadow back again, filled with a menagerie of hens, rabbits and geese as well as sheep!

To learn more...

Clean air is essential for life. Just like Clementine's kingdom, we too have "bubble machines" that pollute our environment. Factories, cars, furnaces, for example, can release harmful gases.

In large cities, pollution is responsible for "smog," a yellow fog that causes respiratory diseases. Pollutants are also responsible for the acid rain that threatens lakes and forests and damages buildings. Certain products cause holes to form in the ozone layer, the gas that encircles the Earth and protects against the sun's harmful rays. And excess carbon dioxide traps the heat, somewhat like the windows of a room exposed to the sun. This warming, or greenhouse effect, could eventually disrupt our climate.

Now that we know more about the dangers of pollution, we are trying to prevent it. Filters are being installed on factory smokestacks and car exhaust systems, for example. People are being encouraged to stop using products that are harmful to the environment. Measures are being taken to preserve our forests. Plants are our allies—they absorb carbon dioxide from the air and store the carbon in their tissues.

Clean air is both free and precious. So let's take care of it!

In the same collection:

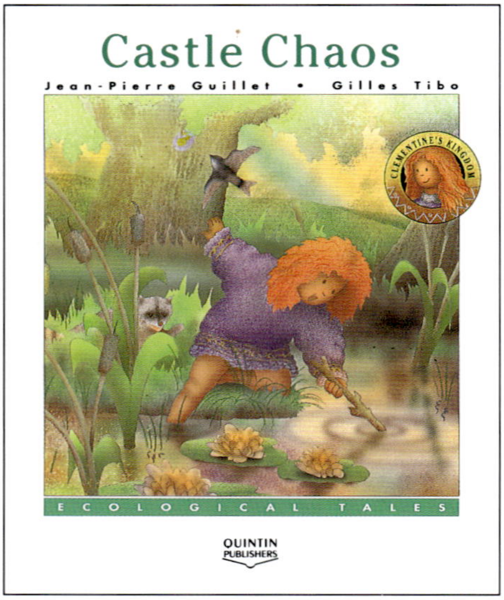